MW01173341

The Bible Chronicles: Birth of a Savior

Robert Jerome Pagan

To my nieces, nephews, and godchildren,

May this book find its way to your hearts, embracing
you with the love with which it was written.

Contents

Title Page

Dedication

Introduction

Chapter 1   1

Chapter 2   9

Chapter 3   18

Chapter 4   26

Chapter 5   36

Chapter 6   42

Chapter 7   47

Chapter 8   56

Chapter 9   60

Chapter 10   66

Chapter 11   71

Chapter 12   76

About The Author   79

Introduction

In our contemporary society, discussing a profound connection to the Divine and the spiritual guidance that shapes our moral compass often draws skepticism. It seems we, as Christians and Catholics, have veered away from acknowledging the supernatural and the spiritual realm that permeates our existence. In this reluctance, we risk harsh judgment through the narrow lens of the earthly realm.

True scholars of the Bible comprehend that belief in the miracles of Jesus is inseparable from acknowledging the treacheries of the devil. The duality of good and evil extends beyond the realm of human actions, delving into the supernatural, marked by decisions made by people ages ago. As time unfolds, intertwining stories and historical accounts of Jesus' era with the ongoing ability to bridge mythology into history, I felt compelled, like any devoted believer, to spread the word of the Lord and celebrate His gift to humanity.

This novel, the inaugural installment in my biblical series, amalgamates years of cultural anthropology, religious studies, Catholic studies, and unwavering faith. My challenge was to craft a narrative that seamlessly integrates historical and biblical references, presenting them in an honest and authentic manner for the enjoyment of a modern audience unafraid to confront the discrepancies in ancient traditions.

I invite you to explore this work not as a testament, but as a companion that offers insights into a challenging era through the eyes of a child on the brink of adulthood. Let skepticism dissipate, and embrace the belief in miracles, for it is faith that will guard us and herald the return of the King of all Kings.

Chapter 1

A Boy Named Jeremiah

T he golden orb of the sun dipped low, a molten sphere descending in a slow dance, casting its farewell glow upon the cobblestone streets of Nazareth. As the sunlight ebbed, warm hues spilled across the town, transforming its narrow thoroughfares into a canvas of amber and crimson. The air buzzed with energy, the hum of life felt like a lively community.

In the midst of this vibrant scene stood Jeremiah, a spirited 12-year-old boy whose presence seemed to be infused with the very essence of the setting sun. His unruly brown hair caught the last rays of daylight, creating a halo that framed his inquisitive eyes. Jeremiah's steps echoed through the narrow streets, each footfall a note in the symphony of activity that enveloped Nazareth.

With the waning light, the juxtaposition of Jeremiah's spirited presence against the backdrop of the town's age-old traditions became even more pronounced. It was a convergence, a fleeting moment suspended in the amber glow—a snapshot of a boy on the brink of discovery, eager to unravel the mysteries that lay beyond the confines of the narrow streets.

Nazareth, a town steeped in humility, unfolded its ancient arms as a haven for devoted followers of Yahweh. The town's heartbeat was the pulse of spirituality, a rhythm that bound the people together in a tapestry of shared faith.

The elders, venerable figures with weathered faces etched with the lines of wisdom, gathered in secluded corners to discuss matters of profound significance. In hushed tones, they spoke of the imminent crossroads that loomed in Jeremiah's path, a juncture where the weight of tradition and the promise of his own destiny converged. The town's traditions, like ancient scrolls unfurled through time, pressed upon Jeremiah's young shoulders.

The elders outlined two distinct paths—the pastoral life, a continuation of a time-honored tradition where Jeremiah would tend to his own herd, echoing the footsteps of generations before him. Alternatively, there was the scholarly path, a journey into the intricate teachings of the Torah within the revered temple, a route paved by the footsteps of fine men who had delved into the sacred scriptures.

As Jeremiah meandered through the streets, the gravity of the decisions awaiting him settled like a tangible presence. The labyrinthine pathways seemed to symbolize the complex choices he would soon confront. Each person he passed played a role in Nazareth, a community where threads of duty, tradition, and individual destinies were interwoven.

Not far from the pulsating heart of Nazareth, atop a hill, bathed in the soft glow of the setting sun, stood the homes of the Roman families—a stoic presence overlooking the spirited town below. From their elevated perch, the Romans observed with a quiet detachment the rituals and customs of the townsfolk. Their homes, nestled against the backdrop of the azure sky, became silent witnesses to the ebb and flow of life in Nazareth. This hillside vantage point offered them a panorama of the sacred practices of the devoted followers of Yahweh, a tableau that hinted at the broader world beyond the confines of this humble town.

Despite the proximity, the Romans maintained a respectful distance, allowing the followers of Yahweh to immerse themselves in their sacred routines undisturbed, as long as taxes were paid. The two communities existed side by side, yet there was an invisible boundary that demarcated the sanctity of Nazareth from the more worldly inclinations of those dwelling on the hill. Laughter of Roman children reached Jeremiah's ears. The laughter served as a bridge, spanning the gap between worlds and whispering of shared humanity beneath the surface differences.

Jeremiah has reached his home and his contemplation continues. Jeremiah retraced the steps of his ancestors through the intricate family tree of the Jewish sons of David. The parchment, worn by the hands of generations, unfolded before him like a sacred manuscript. Each name etched into the delicate fibers of the paper told a story—a story whispered through time and bound by the threads of heritage.

His connection to this storied lineage was both a source of profound pride and a tether linking him to the ancestral past. The names of his forebears were not just ink on parchment; they were echoes of resilience, of trials endured and triumphs celebrated. In the quiet confines of his home, Jeremiah's thoughts swirled with the pride of ancestors long gone, their stories becoming the foundation upon which his own journey would unfold.

As he reflected on the tribulations his people had weathered, Jeremiah found himself drawn to the window. The city of Nazareth, bathed in the glow of twilight, seemed to shimmer with an ethereal light. It was as if a celestial hand had reached down from the heavens, casting a luminous sign upon the town—a silent promise of change, of miracles waiting on the horizon.

The notion of a Messiah, a figure whispered about

in tales of old, echoed in the hearts of the faithful. Since childhood, Jeremiah had harbored a profound sense that the era of miracles and transformation was imminent, a belief instilled in him by the stories passed down through generations.

"Jeremiah!" his father's voice rang out, breaking through the hushed atmosphere. "Come, your cousin has joined us this evening for Sabbath."

The call snapped Jeremiah from his contemplation, and with a sense of anticipation, he made his way into the heart of the home. His cousin, Joseph, awaited—a seasoned carpenter whose skill resonated through the wooden creations of Nazareth. Joseph, soon to be wed to Mary, the woman of exquisite beauty whose lineage could be traced back to the first man of the Garden, Adam.

Jeremiah's pulse quickened at the prospect of family gathered in prayer. Joseph, older and more experienced, stood as a symbol of guidance.

"Jeremiah," his father beckoned once more, "your cousin awaits. Let us join in prayers, for tonight, the air feels charged with a promise, as if the whispers of our ancestors are carried on the winds of change."

With a swift nod, Jeremiah moved to greet his cousin, ready to partake in the sacred rituals that bound their family and town together. The anticipation in the air, combined with the timeless echoes of his lineage, created a palpable sense of expectancy—a feeling that, perhaps, the time of change and miracles was indeed at hand.

Over 2,000 miles away, far beyond the majestic pyramids of Egypt and into the vast lands where the descendants of the first man's son dwelled, a group of devout followers of Yahweh, believers in the sacred stories of the Torah. On the banks of the Red Sea, a sacred gathering unfolded, as three kings from the tribes of the Magi, the wise men of the East, came together for a momentous meeting.

The men, known as Melchior, Jasper, and Balthazar, sat beneath the vast expanse of the star-studded sky. The very same sky that had, on this night years ago, bestowed upon them a vision so profound that it sent shivers down their spines. They were foretold of the conception of a King of all Kings, a divine event that held the promise of reshaping the course of history.

In homage to the divine revelation, the three kings kindled a sacred fire, its flames dancing in rhythmic harmony with the night breeze. A ram, symbolizing the ancient sacrifice made by Abraham in lieu of his first son, was offered as a burnt offering. The scent of the smoldering embers waned through the air, a fragrant tribute to the stories woven into the fabric of their shared faith.

As the embers flickered and the men sat in solemn contemplation, the air around them became charged with spiritual energy. It was then that a vision, a voice from the heavens, graced their gathering. The voice spoke of a divine mission—to prepare, to gather their possessions, and to embark on a journey northward. In two weeks' time, they were to set forth, carrying riches from their respective tribes, for they were destined to meet the King of all Kings, the Son of God.

With a profound sense of purpose, Melchior, Jasper, and Balthazar raised their cups in a solemn toast, their words of praise ascending to the heavens. Each sip was a communion with the divine, a celebration of the shared vision that bound them together on this sacred night.

As they looked toward the horizon, the promise of a sign from God, a celestial guidepost, lingered in the air.

The starry expanse above seemed to twinkle, and the three kings knew that their journey was not only a physical pilgrimage but a spiritual quest guided by the divine hand.

In the quiet solitude of her chamber, a young woman named Mary found herself in a reflective state. Her thoughts billow around the impending betrothal to Joseph and the sacred duty that awaited her—the duty that women gathered to discuss in hushed tones each month. As a participant in this revered space of women, Mary now bore the responsibility of providing future sons of David, a weighty duty that filled with the echoes of generations.

In the midst of her thoughts, the room suddenly filled with an ethereal light, transforming the darkness into an otherworldly radiance. Before Mary stood a celestial being, a winged messenger of Yahweh. Far from instilling fear, the presence of this divine envoy enveloped Mary with a sense of profound comfort.

"I am Gabriel, sent from the one true God to bear you a message," declared the celestial being. Mary, stunned by the proclamation, sat in quiet, her heart echoing with a mixture of reverence and curiosity.

"You have found favor with our Lord, Mary. For this, he will bless you, and you will conceive a son," Gabriel announced, his words imbued with a sacred weight.

Puzzled by the celestial announcement, Mary questioned, "How am I to have a child? I have never laid with a man, nor have I joined the women until tonight."

With an assurance that transcended the earthly realm, Gabriel responded, "God has placed His divine presence within you and has bestowed upon you His son —the King of all men, the Son of our Lord. You shall name him Jesus, and he will reign for all of eternity, seated at the right hand of God."

In that sacred moment, Mary felt the undeniable truth of Gabriel's words coursing through her being. The power of God grew within her, a sensation that she could not deny. Though questions swirled within her, Mary hesitated to voice them, recognizing the divine purpose unfolding within her, a purpose that would shape the course of history and weave her destiny into the grand tapestry of sacred narratives.

Chapter 2

A Man Like No Other

T he three wise men, Melchior, Jasper, and Balthazar, had dispersed back to their respective tribes after their solemn meeting on the banks of the Red Sea. Their hearts brimmed with purpose as they embarked on a mission to gather precious gifts for the newborn King, the long-awaited Messiah whose arrival had been foretold by the celestial skies.

Weeks passed, and the vision spread among the tribes and grew like the flame of a sacred fire. The air buzzed with whispered excitement, as each man and woman awaited the return of the wise men who held the promise of a divine revelation.

The three kings, driven by a profound sense of duty and guided by their unwavering faith, diligently collected treasures befitting a King of all Kings. They gathered gold, symbolizing royalty and majesty; frankincense, an aromatic resin offered in homage to the divine; and myrrh, a precious gift associated with sacrifice and the anointing of kings.

As the time for their return approached, the three men reconvened at the banks of the Red Sea, the very place where their journey had begun. The air was thick with anticipation, and the night sky sparkled above them, mirroring the countless stars that had guided their vision.

They stood on the precipice of a journey not defined by maps or known routes, but rather by the compass of faith. The path ahead, a pilgrimage into the unknown, where each step would be guided by the divine hand.

The journey northward was not merely a physical passage; it was a proclamation to all the children of the tribes of Israel. It was an opportunity to herald the arrival of the long-awaited Messiah, a momentous occasion that transcended the boundaries of individual tribes and united the diverse people under the banner of a shared prophecy.

Jeremiah, amidst the vast expanse of the fields, was absorbed in the quiet rhythm of his shepherd duties when an unsettling disturbance reverberated through the town. The once harmonious sounds of the community were drowned out by loud excitement, the air pulsating with calls for banishment and stoning. The fervor was so intense that it cut through the very fabric of a town that had always been characterized by a deep sense of love and unity.

Instinctively, Jeremiah abandoned his shepherd's staff and sprinted towards the source of the uproar, his heart pounding with a mixture of curiosity and trepidation. As he approached, a disconcerting scene unfolded before him— a frenzied mob of holy men encircling a lone figure: Mary.

Accusations were hurled with venom, the once gentle voices of the townsfolk now distorted by anger. Among the crowd, one of the high priests of the temple emerged as a vocal antagonist, his voice cutting through the chaos. He screamed, "Esther has told her husband that you have not joined in the monthly moon cycle of the women. Have you broken your vows?"

The accusation hung heavy in the air, and the onlookers, caught in a maelstrom of emotions, gazed upon Mary with a mixture of curiosity, judgment, and perhaps even sympathy. The weight of the accusation shatters the illusion of the once idyllic town.

Jeremiah, amidst the turmoil, felt a surge of conflicting emotions. He had known Mary as a woman of virtue and kindness, a member of their close-knit community. The sudden turn of events perplexed him, and he couldn't fathom the accusations being leveled against her.

Mary, standing in the center of the storm, faced the barrage of accusations with a stoic calmness. Her gaze, a mixture of resolve and innocence, met the eyes of the gathered crowd.

Like a towering figure amongst men, Joseph surged through the crowd, a forceful presence that cut through the chaos. He positioned himself defiantly in front of Mary, a sight that left Jeremiah in shock. It was an unprecedented act for Joseph to stand against the holy men, a gesture that defied the norms of their community.

"She has done no wrong, no injustice. Leave me to my betrothed, and as the man of my family, I will decide what is to be done!" bellowed Joseph, his voice resonating with an authority that commanded attention. The crowd, taken aback by this unexpected intervention, began to disperse, their fervor dampened by the force of Joseph's resolve.

Jeremiah, a silent observer amidst the dispersing crowd, couldn't help but be awestruck by Joseph's unwavering defense of Mary. The act of shielding her from the accusations, of asserting his authority in the face of the holy men, spoke volumes about Joseph's character. In that moment, as Joseph gently lifted Mary from the ground, his hands delicately brushing away the dirt and mud that had clung to her during the tumultuous encounter, Jeremiah glimpsed a depth of love and care that surpassed any he had witnessed within his own family.

The two figures, Joseph and Mary, stood together in the aftermath of the chaos, a tableau of resilience against the storm of accusations. As Joseph led Mary away,

Jeremiah couldn't tear his eyes from the unfolding scene. The love that bound the couple together seemed to radiate, casting a light that transcended the shadows of doubt and suspicion.

Left amidst the fading crowd, Jeremiah began his journey home, a path marked by a cascade of questions that tumbled through his mind like rivers spread across the land. Why had the people accused Mary, a woman of unwavering virtue? How would Joseph and Mary navigate the aftermath of the town's rage, the remnants of an accusation that had tarnished their names? Most perplexing of all, why had Mary not denied the accusations, especially the one regarding her condition?

In the quiet sanctuary of Joseph's home, a profound stillness settled as he stood, his gaze fixed upon Mary. His eyes, pools of emotion, betrayed the tumultuous storm within his heart—water brimming with the currents of love, confusion, and a quest for understanding.

In a voice that held neither accusation nor anger, Joseph spoke, "Mary, tell me, what am I to do?" His words hung in the air, a plea for guidance, as he sought the truth in the eyes of the woman he loved.

Mary's response, however, came in the form of a prolonged silence. A heavy pause that lingered with the weight of unspoken words. Sensing her internal struggle, Joseph continued, his voice gentle yet laden with the gravity of the situation, "Am I to allow you to be stoned? Should I walk silently away?"

Tears welled in Mary's eyes as she met Joseph's gaze. Her voice, when it finally broke through the silence, carried a sincerity that resonated with a profound truth. "Joseph, I swear to you, I have not broken any vow. THIS child was given to the world." Her admission hung in the air, a declaration that pierced the veil of confusion.

Joseph, torn between the evidence before him and the love he held for Mary, felt a pang of uncertainty. Yet, her honesty, the earnestness in her eyes, stirred something within him. He wanted to believe her, to trust in the love they had shared.

In that moment, Joseph's thoughts turned to Mary's family—a lineage blessed by Yahweh in ways that transcended the ordinary. He recalled the recent miracle bestowed upon Mary's uncle Zacharias and his wife Elizabeth, who, in their old age, had been granted the extraordinary gift of bearing a child. Perhaps, he mused, these past six months were a continuation of divine blessings for Mary's family.

Filled with conflicting emotions and grappling with monumental decisions, Joseph quietly left the confines of the home. Under the celestial glow of the stars, he sought solace and clarity. The heavens above seemed to whisper ancient truths, and Joseph, burdened with the weight of choices, immersed himself in the celestial expanse—a canvas upon which the destiny of a humble carpenter and a virtuous young woman would be painted against the backdrop of divine mysteries.

As Jeremiah's home became a gathering place for concerned men from all corners of the town, the air inside echoed with heated conversations. Voices rose and fell, demanding justice according to the ancient laws of the tribe of Moses. They insisted that Joseph adhere to the stern customs that dictated such matters, asserting that the perceived shameful act committed by Mary should not be allowed to persist.

Jeremiah listened, a sense of bewilderment etched on his face. The cruelty of the accusations against Mary perplexed him, for he knew her to be the most virtuous among the girls in the town. The unfolding events seemed to cast a shadow over the town's once warm embrace, leaving Jeremiah grappling with the stark contrast between the love that once defined their community and the accusatory fervor that now threatened to tear it apart.

Joseph continued his solitary journey under the watchful gaze of the olive trees. The rhythmic rustle of leaves and the soothing whispers of the wind accompanied him as he sought refuge beneath the branches of an ancient olive tree. As the sounds of nature embraced him, Joseph immersed himself in prayer and contemplation.

In the hushed moments of reprieve, sleep gently cradled Joseph in its embrace. It was then, beneath the ancient olive tree, that his dreams became a conduit for divine intervention. In the realm of slumber, Joseph found himself visited by the angelic presence of Gabriel.

"Joseph, son of David, do not be afraid to take Mary your wife into your home," the angel's voice resonated through the dream. "For it is through the Holy Spirit that this child has been conceived in her. She will bear a son, and you are to name him Jesus, because he will save his people from their sins."

With these celestial words, Joseph awoke. The clarity and assurance bestowed upon him in the dream settled deep within his soul. No longer burdened by doubt, Joseph felt a resolute conviction to stand by Mary, to be wed to her, and to embrace the divine purpose that unfolded before them.

Upon returning to the town, Joseph carried within him the weight of the divine message bestowed upon him in the dream. The whispers of the olive trees seemed to linger in his ears as he walked with purpose, the path ahead now illuminated by a clarity that transcended the confusion of the previous days.

As he approached Jeremiah's home, the air was thick with tension. The conversations that had filled the space were a distant murmur, yet the gravity of the accusations against Mary lingered. Joseph, fortified by the celestial guidance he had received, entered the house with a quiet determination.

The gathered men turned their eyes toward Joseph, their faces a mix of curiosity and expectation. Jeremiah, caught in the crossfire of communal judgment, met Joseph's gaze, silently conveying the complex emotions that danced in the air.

In a calm yet unwavering voice, Joseph addressed the assembly. "Mary has done no wrong. The child she carries is conceived through the Holy Spirit, and we are to name him Jesus, for he will save his people from their sins." The words, charged with a divine certainty, hung in the air, challenging the accusations that had cast a shadow over Mary's virtue.

The men, grappling with the unexpected turn of events, exchanged uneasy glances. The air in the room seemed to shift, as if the very fabric of reality was being rewoven. Joseph's conviction, rooted in the ethereal guidance of his dream, radiated with a quiet strength that demanded acknowledgment.

Jeremiah, standing amidst the gathering, felt a surge of relief and awe. The divine purpose that had been unveiled to Joseph echoed through the room, challenging the rigid expectations of the town. In that moment, the air became charged with the recognition that they were witnessing the unfolding of something extraordinary.

The echoes of the celestial guidance still resonating

within him, Joseph returned home to find Mary, her eyes reflecting a mix of weariness and resilience. In the quiet sanctuary of their shared space, they sat down to discuss the tumultuous events that had unfolded in Nazareth.

The air, thick with unspoken emotions, carried the weight of their shared journey. Joseph, with a gentle yet firm demeanor, began, "Mary, it is clear that our presence here has stirred unrest in the town. Perhaps it is best for you to go to Ein Kerem, to help your uncle Zacharias and Aunt Elizabeth in bringing their son into the world."

Mary, thoughtful and composed, nodded in agreement. The prospect of assisting in the birth of her cousin held a sacred significance, offering a respite from the judgmental eyes of Nazareth. It was a decision made not in retreat but in the pursuit of a higher purpose.

"Ein Kerem will provide you solace, Mary," Joseph continued, his words carrying a reassurance that transcended the physical journey. "It will allow the temper of Nazareth to settle, and when you return, we can face whatever lies ahead together."

The decision, though laden with the weight of temporary separation, held the promise of a quieter respite in Ein Kerem. Mary, recognizing the wisdom in Joseph's words, embraced the opportunity to find solace and support within the familial embrace of Zacharias and Elizabeth.

In the days that followed, Mary embarked on the journey to Ein Kerem, carrying with her the hopes of a community grappling with the unconventional circumstances surrounding her pregnancy. As the town of Nazareth settled into a contemplative quiet, Joseph remained steadfast, trusting in the divine plan that had unfolded in his dream.

Chapter 3

A Familiar Home

Herod Antipas reclined on his ornate throne in the opulent palace of Jerusalem, his demeanor as suspicious as the very walls that surrounded him. A Roman appointed as the king of the Jews, Herod wielded power over Galilee and stood as a symbol of Roman authority in the region. The grand walls of the Second Temple in Jerusalem, a testament to his reign, cast a shadow over his troubled countenance.

While Herod reveled in the luxury of his palace, he was acutely aware of the precarious position he occupied. His kingship and the longevity of his family's reign were but threads woven into the intricate tapestry of the Roman Empire. Herod's success hinged on the compliance and taxation of his subjects, and he knew that any misstep could unravel the fragile stability he had worked to maintain.

In this intricate dance of power, a message arrived from Tiberius Julius Caesar Augustus, the formidable Emperor of Rome. The edict conveyed a directive – a census was to be conducted. The very mention of a census stirred Herod's ire, for it was not merely a count of his subjects but a catalyst for unrest and disruption in his kingdom.

To conduct an accurate census, Herod faced a dilemma. The people were required to return to their ancestral homes, a decree that would unsettle the peace and disrupt the established order. The prospect of upheaval loomed large, as men across the kingdom would be compelled to abandon their daily lives and embark on a journey back to their familial roots.

Herod's contempt for the census was rooted in the

inherent challenge it posed to his rule. The disruption it would bring to the daily lives of his subjects, coupled with the potential for dissent, threatened to undermine the fragile stability he had painstakingly built. Yet, his compliance with the Emperor's command was not optional; it was a binding obligation that hung over him like a sword.

As Herod contemplated the implications of the impending census, the palace walls seemed to close in around him. His reign rested in the delicate balance between appeasing the Roman overlords and managing the expectations of his subjects.

Ein Kerem, an ancient city nestled among the rolling hills of Judea. The air was rich with the scent of blooming flowers and the timeless tales that whispered through the olive groves. Ein Kerem, seemed frozen in time, an ode to the history that had unfolded within its embrace.

Upon a hillside, a lovely estate and vineyard lay cradled in the arms of nature. The vines, heavy with clusters of grapes, sprawled gracefully across the landscape. The estate, a haven tucked into the side of the hill, boasted an enchanting view of the surrounding valley. The stone walls, weathered by time, spoke of generations who had tended to the land and nurtured its bounty.

Two months had passed since Mary arrived at the home of her maternal uncle, Zacharias. The estate, with its rustic charm, had become a sanctuary for her weary soul. The vineyard, a quilt of green and purple, painted a picturesque scene against the backdrop of ancient hills.

In the heart of the estate, Mary found her aunt, Elizabeth, a woman of 60 years, her resilience etched into the lines of her face. The bonds between Mary and Elizabeth were forged not only through familial ties but also through the shared acknowledgment of the divine gifts bestowed upon them. Elizabeth, despite her age, carried the miracle of impending motherhood—a testament to the wonders that unfolded in Ein Kerem.

Mary, with a heart full of gratitude and a desire to contribute, helped prepare Elizabeth for the challenges that accompanied childbirth. The ancient walls of the estate bounced with the laughter and shared stories of these two women, their spirits entwined in the sacred journey that awaited them.

Mary, who had once lived with her uncle in Ein Kerem, felt a twinge of sadness to find him robbed of the ability to speak. Yet, as she observed the loving connection between Zacharias and Elizabeth, she knew that this old couple, bound by faith and love, would make wonderful parents. Mary envisioned a future where their sons, born in the same season, would grow together, their destinies intertwined in ways that transcended the boundaries of familial ties.

In the quiet sanctuary of Joseph's workshop, the scent of wood shavings and the rhythmic cadence of craftsmanship. Joseph, his hands skilled in the art of carpentry, meticulously crafted an ornate cradle that spoke of love and anticipation. Jeremiah , sat nearby, mesmerized by the dance of Joseph's hands as they shaped the wooden masterpiece.

Over the past month, a subtle transformation had occurred within Jeremiah . The walls that had once separated him from his older cousin seemed to crumble, replaced by a growing sense of love and respect. As he watched Joseph's hands bring the cradle to life, Jeremiah sensed an unspoken depth, a hidden emotion yearning to be released.

Unable to contain his curiosity any longer, Jeremiah ventured into the uncharted territory of emotions. "Do you miss her?" he asked, the question hanging in the air like the delicate scent of freshly cut wood.

Joseph, his eyes focused on the intricate details of the cradle, took a moment before responding. "I worry for her," he confessed, his voice carrying a weight that hinted at the complexities hidden beneath the surface.

Jeremiah, sensing that Joseph desired to unravel the tangle of emotions within, probed further. "Why?" he inquired gently, opening the door to a conversation that had lingered unspoken.

Joseph, pausing in his work, delved into the depths of his thoughts. "I know that after the baby is born, we will have to leave," he explained. The weight of his words hung in the air, and Jeremiah furrowed his brow in confusion.

Joseph continued, revealing the underlying concerns that haunted him. "Not only for Mary's safety but for the safety of the child who will soon come into this world. Between skepticism and fear, I know that no child created in this way would be safe here."

As the truth unfolded, Jeremiah grasped the gravity of Joseph's worries. The unconventional circumstances of Mary's pregnancy, shrouded in skepticism and fear, painted a complex picture of a future fraught with challenges. The ornate cradle, in the process of creation, seemed to carry not only the promise of new life but also the weight of an uncertain journey that lay ahead.

The cry of Roman heralds, echoing through the narrow streets of Nazareth, reached the ears of Joseph and Jeremiah like an unsettling omen. It was a sound not often heard outside of tax season, and its presence outside Joseph's house signaled an uncommon occurrence. Sensing the urgency in the air, both Joseph and Jeremiah hurriedly set aside their work in the workshop and rushed to the door to hear the crier's decree.

As they stepped outside, the Roman emissary, usually a stern tax collector whose visits were met with apprehension, stood in the midst of the bustling town. The crier proclaimed the mandate issued by Herod, a decree that sent ripples of concern through the assembled townsfolk. In five months' time, every man, woman, and child was to comply with a census that required them to return to their ancestral homes for counting. The air hung heavy with the implications of this directive, a mandate that demanded not just obedience but a disruption of the familiar routines that anchored the people of Nazareth.

The news of the census bore a unique weight, for it signified not only the imposition of Roman authority but also the potential upheaval of the town's very fabric. The prospect of families scattering to their ancestral homes, leaving behind the daily rhythms of life in Nazareth, stirred a collective unease among the townspeople.

Joseph's mind raced as he contemplated the implications of the census. The timing, amidst the delicate circumstances surrounding Mary's pregnancy, added an extra layer of complexity to an already challenging situation. The shadows of skepticism and fear, which had cast a pall over Mary and Joseph's journey, deepened with the realization that this census could alter the course of their lives in unforeseen ways.

In the vast expanse of the sand-soaked desert, the glow of a campfire flickered, casting dancing shadows on the faces of those gathered around. Balthazar, with a twinkle in his eyes, regaled a captivated audience of children and their parents with the timeless tale of

David and Goliath. As the daylight began to fade, the air resonated with the awe-struck whispers of the listeners, their imaginations ignited by the vivid narrative of courage and triumph.

Balthazar's animated storytelling transported the eager listeners to a realm where a shepherd's sling became a weapon of righteousness, and a giant's pride crumbled in the face of unwavering faith. The children's eyes widened, and the parents found themselves captivated by the enchanting narrative woven by the wise traveler.

Just as the echoes of David's victory lingered in the desert air, Melchior, the elder among the three Magi, interjected with a powerful thunder of his own. He began to recount the remarkable story of Moses and the sacred celebration of Passover. The desert night became a canvas for his words, each syllable carrying the weight of ancient history.

Melchior's storytelling transcended the boundaries of time, transporting the listeners to the very heart of the Exodus, where a sea parted to make way for freedom. The flickering flames of the campfire danced in harmony with the rhythm of his words, and the faces around him reflected a shared sense of wonder and reverence.

As the narrative unfolded, the desert breeze seemed to carry the scent of freedom and redemption. The story of Passover resonated not just as a historical event but as a timeless testament to the enduring spirit of hope and liberation.

Amidst the lingering echoes of Moses's journey, Jasper, the third of the wise men, began to speak. His voice, a steady and soothing presence, spoke of a story that transcended all others—the story of the soon-to-be-born King of all Kings, the true Messiah.

Jasper's words held a sacred promise, a prophecy that had brought them together on this journey through the vast expanse of the desert. The campfire flickered in anticipation as he spoke of the miraculous birth that awaited them, a birth destined to herald a new era of hope, redemption, and the fulfillment of prophecies.

The gathering, bathed in the warmth of the desert night, listened with bated breath as Jasper painted a vision of a future where the footsteps of the true Messiah would echo through the corridors of time. In that moment, beneath the starlit canopy of the desert sky, a shared understanding dawned on those who gathered—an understanding that their journey held a purpose far greater than the tales of the past. They were pilgrims in a divine narrative, bound by destiny to witness the unfolding of a story that would shape the very fabric of their existence.

Chapter 4

John

J eremiah sat, wearied by the journey. His father, mother, and Joseph had entrusted him with the important task of bringing Mary back from her uncle's house, especially now as the time for the birth of Elizabeth's baby approached. The responsibility weighed on his shoulders, marking the first time he ventured into the world on his own.

As he embarked on the over-a-day's travel, the vastness of Galilee unfolded before him. Excitement and anticipation danced in his eyes as he realized that Nazareth, his little village, was not the only haven for the people of Yahweh. The revelation struck him, and he almost chuckled at the smallness of his previous perspective. The land of Galilee, with its varied landscapes and vibrant communities, overwhelmed him with the realization that there was a broader world beyond the familiar confines of Nazareth.

In the midst of this realization, a profound connection to his ancestors, those who had journeyed with Moses in search of the promised land, swept over Jeremiah. Though lacking a true understanding of the hardships they endured, he could only imagine that this sense of discovery and wonder mirrored what they might have felt. The echoes of his forebears walking through the vastness of the land, searching for the land of Israel, resonated in his childlike mind.

Thoughts of his father and Joseph giving him advice before setting out replayed in his mind, grounding him in the purpose of his journey. He stood up, renewed with a sense of determination, his eyes fixed on the path leading to the home of Zacharias.

The rhythmic thud of camel hoofs against the desert floor marked the triumphant arrival of the Magi on the outskirts of Samaria. Overcome with joy and relief from the trials of their arduous journey, the caravan came to a halt as the oldest of the Magi, Melchior, raised his hand, demanding a pause. His wise eyes, weathered by time and illuminated by a deep inner knowing, scanned the heavens.

A gentle star floated across the night sky—a celestial beacon that, to the untrained eye, might be dismissed as an average shooting star. Yet, for these men, it was a divine sign, a celestial whisper urging them to seek rest and reprieve. The weariness that clung to their aging bodies, after a month and a half of travel, resonated in the throbbing of their feet.

Balthazar, ever the jester of the trio, quipped that it must be a glorious thing not to have to live as long as the men of ancient times. Laughter, hearty and well-earned, echoed in the stillness of the night. Yet, beneath the jest, there lingered a shared understanding that their journey held a significance far beyond the physical toll it exacted.

Jasper, with a solemn pride, reminded his companions that their travels were not solely for the purpose of meeting the awaited Savior but also to spread the word of their people. He spoke of the necessity to gather followers, a following that this young king would need to conquer the sins of the world.

As the men settled into contemplation, Melchior pondered the profound questions that loomed over their quest. Could this be the Messiah destined to free the Children of Yahweh? Would the tribes of David, Jacob, and Abraham find liberation, and would Israel finally become the home for all Jews, governed by this new king?

In a moment almost too timely to be coincidental, the desert air responded to Melchior's musings. A small sand tornado spiraled around him, lifting his staff from his hand. The two other Magi exchanged a knowing glance, a silent acknowledgment that questioned not the will of God but affirmed their duty to spread the message entrusted to them by divine messengers.

With that subtle yet powerful reminder, the Magi ceased their ponderings, offering prayers and gratitude under the star-strewn sky. They lay down to rest in the soft desert sands, the anticipation of the next morning's journey guiding their dreams.

Jeremiah's peaceful slumber in the alcove of a rock was abruptly shattered by the sounds of violence. Startled and frightened, he peered around the rock to witness a disturbing scene: Roman soldiers mercilessly beating an elderly Jewish man. The demand for payment to use the road served as a painful reminder of the harsh reality of racism and hatred that lurked beyond the sheltered walls of his village.

Shocked and conflicted, Jeremiah, shielded from such blatant injustice in his sheltered life, held his breath, contemplating the weight of the moment. The desire to rush forward and intervene surged within him, but an invisible force seemed to pull him back. A gentle yet firm hand, unseen by mortal eyes, restrained him, compelling him to stay put. It was as if the divine hand of God held him back, urging him not to intervene.

With a heavy heart, Jeremiah watched as the Roman soldiers callously left the bloodied elderly man in the street, a victim of their brutal and discriminatory attack. Gritting his teeth in frustration, Jeremiah approached the man, offering him water and compassion. He asked about the man's destination, and with a kindred sense of purpose, he discovered that they were headed in the same direction.

With genuine concern, Jeremiah proposed walking together to ensure the man's safety, even suggesting that they spend the night at his camp. The battered man, introduced as Ariel, gratefully accepted the offer. As they shared a makeshift camp, Ariel's story unfolded, revealing that he, too, was on his way to visit Zacharias.

Jeremiah, captivated by the tale of Zacharias, leaned in with keen interest, urging Ariel to recount the unfolding miracle with more detail. Ariel, sensing Jeremiah's eagerness, continued the narrative.

Ariel narrated how Zacharias, in the sacred precincts of the temple, was chosen by lot to perform the revered duty of offering incense to God—a task he believed to be the closest he would ever be to the divine presence. In the solemnity of the moment, as Zacharias prepared the incense offering, he prayed fervently, recognizing the hand of God guiding him.

As Ariel painted the scene, he described the hallowed encounter with the Archangel Gabriel. The celestial messenger revealed to Zacharias the divine plan: that Elizabeth, despite her advanced age, would conceive a child. This child, named John, would herald the coming of the Messiah, preparing the way for the fulfillment of ancient prophecies. Ariel emphasized the magnitude of the moment, detailing how Gabriel's words echoed with the promise of miracles that would soon unfold.

Jeremiah, hanging on every word, urged Ariel to reveal what happened next. Ariel's voice carried the weight of the unfolding drama as he recounted how Zacharias, despite the extraordinary revelation, faltered in his faith. The old priest questioned the feasibility of his elderly wife bearing a child, prompting Gabriel to take decisive action.

In a moment of divine consequence, Gabriel silenced Zacharias, stripping him of his ability to speak. The very breath held in that sacred space seemed to be snatched away as Zacharias, in that profound instant, lost his voice. Ariel described the shock and awe that filled the temple as Zacharias emerged, mute, leaving the assembled men in bewilderment.

Undeterred, Zacharias, unable to speak, communicated the miraculous encounter by inscribing the divine message on a tablet. The men of the temple, though puzzled, respected the sacred nature of Zacharias's revelation.

The story unfolded further as Ariel narrated the passing of nine months, leading to the moment when Elizabeth, against all odds, was ready to birth the prophesied miracle. Jeremiah, his heart filled with wonder and anticipation, absorbed the tale with a profound sense of gratitude for the miracles woven into the fabric of his homeland.

As Ariel concluded the account, Jeremiah, touched by the divine narrative, bid Ariel a good night, drifting into a peaceful sleep. In the realm of dreams, the messengers of God continued to weave their tales, bringing the promise of miracles that transcended the boundaries of age, doubt, and silence.

The night air was filled with the visceral sounds of Elizabeth's labor, her anguished cries echoing beyond the confines of the sacramental tent. The atmosphere painted with urgency as a procession of women moved in and out of the tent, their arms laden with water and cloth, their faces etched with a mixture of determination and compassion. The men, gathered around the fire, sat in a collective stillness, their faces reflecting the weight of God's gift.

Amidst the hushed whispers and the distant wails of Elizabeth's pain, Zacharias, the father-to-be, sat among the men, his contemplative gaze fixed on the flickering flames. His mind teemed with conflicting emotions—gratitude for the miraculous gift bestowed upon him by Yahweh and worry for his aged wife enduring the rigors of childbirth. Yet, a steadfast faith anchored him, for he knew the protective hand of the Lord would guide Elizabeth through this sacred journey, just as it had for the women of his ancestral lineage.

As the firelight danced on Zacharias's face, the rhythmic chaos of the birthing tent continued, a symphony of life and struggle that transcended the boundaries of the mundane. The men shared silent glances, their thoughts intertwined with the unseen divine providence.

Mary, in the advanced stages of her own pregnancy, her belly swollen with six and a half months of growth, sat drenched in sweat. In a moment of respite, she reached up to her uncle, Zacharias, her voice a tender whisper. Assuring him with unwavering faith, she spoke of Elizabeth's blessed state, drawing a parallel to her own miraculous conception. The shared understanding between Mary and Zacharias, a communion of faith and divine connection, held them in a sacred bond, transcending the palpable tension in the air.

The first rays of dawn painted the sky over the valley as Jeremiah and Ariel reached the home of Zacharias and Elizabeth. The timeliness of their arrival seemed almost scripted, synchronized with the crescendo of cheers emanating from the sacramental tent where the women were gathered. The joyous celebration, punctuated by exclamations of happiness, propelled Jeremiah and Ariel forward as they sprinted towards the source of the commotion.

As they approached the tent, the veil of worry momentarily lifted from Zacharias' face, replaced by an eager anticipation. The air was charged with a mix of excitement and anxiety, as if the very elements conspired to create an unforgettable moment.

Mary, the herald of glad tidings, emerged from the tent, her face radiant with joy. She addressed Zacharias with familial affection, proclaiming the birth of a son, a testament to the truth of God's word. Despite the elation, a flicker of concern crossed Zacharias' eyes, prompting a silent inquiry about Elizabeth's well-being. Mary, in response, offered a gentle nod, signaling the safe arrival of the newborn.

With a heart brimming with joy and a stride quickened by the anticipation of the miracle within, Zacharias entered the tent to reunite with his wife. Though the ability to speak had been taken from him, his gestures and expressions spoke volumes of his overflowing gratitude.

Outside the tent, a gathering crowd clamored for the announcement of the newborn's name. Mary, bearing the honor bestowed upon her by Elizabeth, declared that the chosen name was John. The proclamation, seemingly innocuous, sent ripples of tension through the assembled men. Their voices rose in protest, asserting that tradition demanded the child be named after his father, Zacharias.

The air became charged with dissent as the men insisted that the child must be named Zacharias, the firstborn son carrying the legacy of their family. The choice of the name John was deemed an insult to their familial traditions.

As Zacharias emerged from the tent, greeted by the crowd that had moments ago celebrated the miraculous birth, he demanded his tablet. With deliberate strokes, he inscribed the words, "My son shall be named John." A profound shift occurred as if the divine hand reached down to touch their gathering. The air warmed, and Zacharias' voice, previously silenced, echoed with newfound resonance. In a declaration that resonated through the villa and the hearts of those gathered, Zacharias proclaimed, "My son is John, and he will herald the King of all Kings, the Messiah, our Savior." The tension evaporated, replaced by a sense of awe and reverence for the divine unfolding within their midst. The echoes of Zacharias' proclamation lingered in the air, a testament to the miraculous power of faith and the divine orchestration of destiny.

The vibrant atmosphere of Ein Kerem, Jeremiah found himself immersed in the rich tapestry of ancient customs and traditions that defined the essence of his people. The jubilation of celebration and the resonance of joyful voices filled the air as the community gathered to partake in rituals that connected them to their shared history.

As the festivities unfolded, Jeremiah marveled at the sacredness woven into each ceremony, from the rhythmic dances to the symbolic rituals that celebrated their identity as a people of Yahweh. One of the significant moments during this celebration was the observance of the covenant with Yahweh through the Jewish rite of circumcision, a solemn tradition that marked the covenant between God and the descendants of Abraham. Jeremiah stood witness to this sacred act, acknowledging the deep spiritual significance it held for the community.

In the ensuing three days of revelry and reflection, Jeremiah forged connections with the members of Mary's extended family. He shared laughter, stories, and moments of prayer, feeling a sense of belonging within this extended kinship.

As the celebration drew to a close, Jeremiah felt a gentle tug within, a reminder that it was time to embark on the journey back to Nazareth. The upcoming travels were twofold – to reunite Mary with Joseph and to prepare for the arduous journey to Bethlehem for the impending census.

With gratitude and warmth, Jeremiah bid farewell to the newfound friends and family in Ein Kerem. The road ahead promised challenges, yet it also held the promise of divine purpose and the unfolding of a destiny that extended beyond the confines of their immediate lives. The journey back to Nazareth held a sense of urgency, a call to prepare for the next chapter in the divine narrative that had intertwined their lives. As he set out on the familiar path, Jeremiah carried with him the echoes of celebration, the warmth of community, and the duty to protect Mary from any harm, because he knew now his soon to be cousin was the Savior of his people.

Chapter 5

Festival of Lights

" In the era of the Second Temple, a time when the weight of oppression bore down heavily on the Jewish people, a ruler named Antiochus IV sought to extinguish the flame of our faith. His despotic rule aimed to replace our sacred traditions with Hellenistic practices, culminating in the desecration of the Holy Temple in Jerusalem. In this sacred space, he offered impure animals and erected an idol, attempting to snuff out the divine light that had illuminated our hearts for generations.

Fueled by an unwavering commitment to our faith, a group of rebels emerged – the Maccabees. Led by the courageous Judah Maccabee, we embarked on a perilous journey marked by guerrilla warfare and an unyielding devotion to the principles that defined our identity. With faith in our hearts, we faced a formidable adversary, fighting against overwhelming odds to reclaim the sanctity of our sacred space.

The climax of our struggle unfolded during the rededication of the Holy Temple. As we sought to purify and consecrate the desecrated sanctuary, we encountered a seemingly insurmountable challenge – a lone flask of ritually pure oil for the sacred menorah, the seven-branched candelabrum symbolizing the eternal light of God. Undeterred by the scarcity of resources, we kindled the menorah with this modest supply of oil. Miraculously, the oil that should have sufficed for only one day burned brightly for eight consecutive days, a divine intervention that allowed us to prepare new, untainted oil." Joseph spoke, filling the house with the Divine.

The house resonated with the sacred lullaby of

prayer, "Blessed are you, Our God, Ruler of the Universe, who makes us holy through Your commandments, and commands us to light the Hanukkah lights." The house sang together.

Jeremiah sat in the dim light, the flickering flames of the menorah casting shadows across the room. His gaze was fixed on his cousin Joseph, who meticulously attended to the candles. The past month had been a cascade of trials and tribulations, and the weight of it all pressed heavily upon Jeremiah's young shoulders.

In the quiet moments, memories of his parents, taken by the relentless sickness that had swept through Nazareth like a merciless tide, flooded Jeremiah's mind. The great sickness, a shadow that originated from the heart of Rome, had stolen away the comforting figures of his family, leaving him, just on the cusp of his bar mitzvah, as a boy bereft of parental guidance.

A haunting guilt lingered within him, for the very days he had spent in Ein Kerem, seeking solace and family warmth, were the days that Nazareth had succumbed to the merciless grip of the plague. His trip to Ein Kerem, in a twist of fate, became the fortuitous shield that preserved his life.

Now, alone in the world, Jeremiah knew that he had to prepare for a journey of his own. The looming census, a testament to his transition into manhood, beckoned him. He would be recorded among the men, standing as a solitary figure in the census, a symbol of survival in the face of loss and a pledge to carry the torch of his lineage forward.

As Joseph completed the lighting of the menorah, the warm glow filled the room, casting a sense of both solace and determination upon Jeremiah's face. The flickering flames reflected the resilience within him, a flame that, despite the shadows of sorrow, burned steadily as he readied himself for the journey that awaited – a journey to be recorded as a man in the census, a journey that would carve his path into the tapestry of his people's history.

In the shadows of the Hanukkah celebration in Jerusalem, where the joyous sounds of the festival echoed through the city, Herod, the king of the Jews, met with his advisors. The flickering lights of the menorah illuminated the grand halls where the ruler deliberated on matters that weighed heavily on his mind.

Fear crept into Herod's heart as news of the impending census reached his ears. The advisors, cognizant of the unease in their king, sought to assuage his concerns. However, in the midst of their discussion, whispers of a prophecy emerged—rumors of the imminent arrival of the king of the Jews.

Herod, a ruler known for his iron grip on power, scoffed at the notion of a rival king. In an air of arrogance, he declared, "There is no king of the Jews, for I am the king of our people!" His laughter echoed through the chambers, masking a tinge of insecurity that lingered within.

His advisors, ever loyal, brought further news. The prophecy, although yet to fully take root among his own people, had begun to spread across the tribes devoted to Yahweh. Concern etched the faces of the king's counselors as they conveyed the growing anticipation surrounding the foretelling of a new king.

In response, Herod, guided by his advisors' counsel, reaffirmed his allegiance to the mighty Emperor in Rome. "The true king we are to fear is the Emperor in Rome," he declared sternly. "The census must be done, and we must ensure our loyalty to Rome remains steadfast." The proclamation hung in the air, a reminder of the delicate balance of power.

Continuing their Hanukkah prayer, the three Magi found themselves in a moment of solitude on the outskirts of Judea, nestled by the flowing waters of the River Jordan. Unlike other nights on their journey, this particular evening held a unique significance as they lit their candles in the gentle glow of the menorah.

The men took delight in a feast they had prepared, breaking challah bread in celebration. The provisions came as gifts from fellow followers and members of their Jewish tribe encountered so far on their journey. Amidst the festive atmosphere, the men couldn't help but silently wonder when they would no longer feel lost and when the promised star would guide them with clarity.

In the stillness of the desert night, the three Magi completed their meal, the flickering flame of the menorah casting dancing shadows around them. As they gazed at the luminous glow, their prayers for guidance seemed to transcend the vast expanse of the desert, carried by the ancient winds that whispered through the dunes.

Then, as if responding to their collective plea, a miraculous event unfolded before their eyes. The flame of the menorah lifted, defying gravity, ascending towards the heavens. It soared into the star-studded sky, its brilliance expanding until it engulfed the entire celestial expanse.

The desert, once bathed in the muted glow of moonlight, now shimmered with an ethereal radiance. The Magi watched in awe as the flame settled, a radiant beacon suspended in the night sky. Its glow was not merely the illumination of fire but a celestial sign, a long-awaited symbol etched in the heavens—a signpost guiding them unerringly toward the fulfillment of prophecy, the discovery of their Messiah.

In the quiet of the desert, the Magi recognized the divine response to their prayers. The radiant beacon hung in the sky like a promise, a luminous guide urging them to embark on the journey that would lead them to the cradle of the newborn King. With a newfound sense of purpose, the Magi eagerly packed their belongings, their hearts alight with the anticipation of the sacred quest ahead. The desert, once a vast and uncertain expanse, now bore witness to the celestial proclamation that would guide these wise men to the revelation of the promised Messiah.

Chapter 6

A Shift In Comfort

A s Jeremy drifted into a deep slumber, a vivid dream enveloped his consciousness, a tapestry of bright colors, ethereal lights, and celestial sounds. Within this dreamworld, the faces of Nephilim and angels danced, each figure telling a story of cosmic struggle and divine order.

The dream unfurled like an ancient scroll, revealing the tale of Lucifer's rebellion and his casting into the darkness. Jeremy witnessed the cosmic upheaval, a drama that unfolded in brilliant hues and shadows.

In the midst of this cosmic narrative, a figure emerged with radiant wings and a countenance of sublime authority—Gabriel, the messenger of God. In the dream, Gabriel addressed Jeremy directly, revealing a divine decree that echoed through the expanse. For the safety of the Savior, the King, Jeremy was instructed to wait three days before embarking on the journey to Bethlehem. Moreover, he was directed not to travel with Joseph and Mary during this period.

As Jeremy awoke from his dream, a sense of bewilderment and awe lingered. The celestial encounter had left an indelible imprint on his soul, and the weight of the divine message pressed upon him. Frightened yet filled with a sacred resolve, he grappled with the extraordinary vision that had unfolded in the realm of dreams. Yet, deep within, he understood that this was a celestial sign, a directive from the divine, and he made a solemn pact with himself to heed God's order.

Nazareth, once a tranquil haven where travelers moved at a leisurely pace, had undergone a stark transformation. The serenity that once graced its fields and pathways had been replaced by an unsettling activity. The air, once filled with the gentle whispers of the wind, now carried the heavy presence of Roman invaders.

The Roman soldiers, with their disciplined march and imposing armor, patrolled the streets, casting an authoritarian shadow over the humble town. The once-familiar faces of the townsfolk were now overshadowed by a wary unease. The peace that Nazareth had known was shattered, replaced by the tension that comes with an occupying force.

The marketplace, where merchants once bartered and laughter echoed, now bore witness to the stern faces of Roman centurions overseeing transactions with a watchful eye. The vibrant tapestry of daily life had frayed, threads unraveling as the people of Nazareth adjusted to the unwelcome intrusion.

Even the sacred spaces, where prayers once ascended in tranquility, now carried the weight of a foreign presence. The Roman invaders seemed oblivious to the spiritual rhythms of the town, their priorities focused solely on asserting control.

Jeremiah was at home, his mind still echoing with the vivid dreams that had visited him the night before. The images of celestial beings and divine proclamations lingered, and a sense of foreboding clung to his thoughts. It was amidst this internal tumult that a distinct knock sounded on his door.

Opening it, he was met with the faces of Joseph and Mary, who stood on his doorstep with a quiet urgency. The purpose of their visit was quickly revealed – the decree for a census had arrived, and Bethlehem, the city of David, beckoned them. Jeremiah's heart sank, for he knew the implications of this journey, especially for Mary, who carried a life within her.

The echoes of his dream resonated in his mind, a celestial command to wait and not travel with Joseph and Mary. Yet, in the face of immediate need, compassion overruled caution. He offered whatever means of transport he could provide –a mule, to spare Mary the arduous journey on foot.

A silent understanding passed between the three of them, an acknowledgment of the unspoken concerns and the shared determination to face the journey together. Heartfelt goodbyes were exchanged, and a plan emerged – to reconvene inside Bethlehem. As the door closed behind them, Jeremiah couldn't shake the sense that this journey held a significance beyond the census, and the threads of fate wove tightly around this trio bound for Bethlehem.

Herod, seated in his palace in Jerusalem, felt a wave of anxiety wash over him. The whispers of the Messiah's imminent arrival had penetrated the walls of his opulent temple, and the tales of the Three Magi crossing his borders in search of the prophesied King of Kings had reached his ears.

The news struck fear into the heart of Herod, the Roman-appointed King of the Jews. He couldn't afford any challenges to his rule, especially not from a potential messiah born to challenge his authority. In response, he swiftly issued orders to his guards and the men of Rome. The directive was clear – find these Three Magi, these bearers of celestial knowledge, and bring them before him.

As Herod's commands echoed through the corridors of power, a sense of urgency gripped the Roman soldiers. Their mission was to suppress any inkling of rebellion, to maintain the dominance of Rome, and to quell any whispers of a new king challenging the established order. The hunt for the Magi had begun, and it was fueled by Herod's fear of losing control over his kingdom.

Chapter 7

A Journey

J oseph and Mary had been on the road for a day, the path congested with families and travelers moving at a pace much swifter than their own. The crowd presented a challenge they hadn't anticipated. As they journeyed, Joseph couldn't shake the feeling that perhaps waiting until after the festival of lights had been a misstep.

The road, usually a familiar companion, felt more chaotic than ever. The divine gift bestowed upon them, the promise of a child who would change the world, served as their inspiration to persevere. Joseph's only wish was for Mary to endure the journey safely, ensuring their son would be born in the comfort of their Nazareth home.

In the midst of their complicated trek, a sudden disturbance interrupted their progress. A snake slithered into their path, startling the mule Mary was riding. The frightened animal reared back, tossing Mary roughly to the ground. Joseph, quick to respond, rushed to her aid, helping her up. Recognizing the need for a respite, they decided to rest for the remainder of the day, seeking refuge from the challenges of the road and the unexpected hurdles that lay ahead.

Running through his house, Jeremiah's urgency was palpable as he searched for the most crucial piece of documentation—a Roman half-tier passport. This single document held the power to distinguish a lawful Roman citizen from others, providing protection against enslavement or servitude. For those without this recognition, the risk of being forced into apparent human trafficking loomed.

Jeremiah's heart swelled with relief as he unearthed

the invaluable paper, hidden underneath some tools that must have been used by his father before he passed away. The memory of his parents flooded his mind, leading Jeremiah to contemplate his actions upon returning from Bethlehem.

Acknowledging the necessity of rest, Jeremiah knew that in just one more day, he would embark on the great journey to meet Joseph and Mary. The anticipation of what lay ahead filled him with a mix of excitement, trepidation, and an unyielding sense of duty.

The night sky, shrouded by dark clouds, cast an inky blackness over the road from Nazareth to Bethlehem. Mary slumbered peacefully next to a crackling fire, tended to by Joseph. As the air whispered secrets, doubts crept into Joseph's mind—not doubts in the miracle, but in his ability to be the right man to raise such an extraordinary child. How would this son of God, born in humble surroundings, perceive Joseph, the simple carpenter?

In the hushed contemplation, the nocturnal silence was disrupted by a subtle sound, slithering through the terrain. Joseph's senses sharpened as the soft slithering drew nearer, eventually growing into a menacing hum. Suddenly, like a horde of malevolent shadows, venomous snakes began converging on Mary with a speed defying human capability.

Reacting swiftly, Joseph seized his staff, positioning himself between his wife and the impending threat. With keen eyes and reflexes, he dipped the staff into the fire, lighting one end. Swinging it like a weapon, he fended off the serpentine onslaught meant for his beloved. As the staff swiped through the air, the clouds above began to part, unveiling the radiant star that had guided the three wise men. A beam of divine light cascaded onto Joseph and Mary's makeshift camp, a celestial force scattering the snakes in retreat, bowing to the power of God's radiant light.

In the mid-morning light, the three Magi were abruptly awoken by the prods of staffs against their encampment. The eldest among them, with a regal air, demanded an explanation for the disturbance of their peaceful slumber. However, these weren't ordinary travelers; they were emissaries of Herod. The men, stern and unyielding, insisted that the Magi gather their belongings and follow them immediately to see Herod. The weight of urgency and authority in their voices left the Magi with no choice but to comply, and so, they prepared to meet with the king.

Jeremiah's gaze lingered on the threshold of his home, a dwelling that echoed with memories of familial warmth now silenced by the passage of time. The door, closing behind him, carried a solemn resonance, marking the beginning of a journey that held both the weight of duty and the echoes of a bygone laughter.

As he stood bathed in the sunlight, Jeremiah could almost feel the comforting presence of his departed parents surrounding him, their spirits woven into the fabric of his being. The memories of shared laughter, tender guidance, and familial love stirred within him, an invisible yet palpable connection that transcended the material world.

A deep breath filled his lungs, and with each exhale, Jeremiah carried the collective wisdom of generations past. The legacy of his ancestors, the stories whispered through time, now propelled him forward. The landscape of Nazareth, familiar yet forever changed, stretched out before him, a canvas on which the tales of his people were painted.

The burden of loss and the responsibility of the journey ahead weighed on Jeremiah's shoulders, yet the indomitable spirit of his lineage propelled him forward. In the face of adversity, he drew strength from the echoes of laughter and the enduring love that defined his family.

In the opulent confines of Herod's palace, the three Magi found themselves in a state of neither imprisonment nor welcome. The air in the room carried tension as they deliberated among themselves, their eyes reflecting the wisdom gained from years of traversing distant lands.

Seated in the chamber, the three men engaged in hushed discussions. Every anecdote and morsel of information they had gathered about the king was dissected, their collective decision crystallizing into a pact of cautious silence.

Balthazar couldn't resist a jest about the relative comfort of their situation, finding solace in the irony that, at least, they were afforded a semblance of rest during the day—coinciding with the time they were compelled to travel. Melchior, with a wry smile, interjected, pondering aloud whether they would indeed be granted the freedom to resume their celestial-guided journey.

Jasper, the anchor of solemnity among them, reminded his companions of the historical precedent of God's chosen enduring imprisonment before fulfilling their divine purpose. The gravity of their mission transcended the luxurious trappings of Herod's palace, and the Magi, undeterred, found strength in the unwavering belief that their journey was part of a greater design.

The plaintive cry of the mule, burdened by the weight of the journey, reached Joseph's ears, prompting him to bring their arduous trek to a temporary halt. Mary, his radiant wife, displayed signs of weariness, her strength tested by the relentless travel. Understanding the pressing need for rest, Joseph chose to seize the opportunity afforded by the weary mule.

As the day's heat persisted, Joseph and Mary decided to embrace the respite. Joseph, who had dutifully maintained watch during the nightly hours, now longed for a brief respite himself. The terrain around them hinted at their proximity to Bethlehem, and Joseph envisioned the benefits of completing their journey under the cool veil of evening.

Selecting a sheltered spot beneath the expanse of the sky, Joseph fashioned a makeshift resting place for his beloved Mary, who settled into a peaceful slumber. The mule, granted a moment of reprieve, grazed contentedly nearby. Joseph, mindful of the precious cargo entrusted to his care, recognized the importance of allowing Mary to rejuvenate.

Lulled by the gentle rustle of leaves and the whispers of a breeze, Joseph, too, succumbed to the embrace of sleep.

Jeremiah moved with a swiftness that seemed to defy the constraints of the earthly realm, the road beneath him a blur as he navigated through a tapestry of scenes—a mosaic of families, soldiers, and the harmonious melodies of nature resonating with the love of the divine. His journey bore the essence of a celestial flight, propelled by a sense of urgency that mirrored the importance of the mission entrusted to him.

As he streaked past the very spot where, just nights before, Joseph and Mary had faced a venomous threat, a shiver of gratitude coursed through Jeremiah. The guardian spirits seemed to whisper their approval, acknowledging the protection granted to the couple under divine providence.

However, his ethereal journey took an abrupt pause as the air thickened with tension. Ahead, a grim tableau unfolded—a group of Roman slave traders, relentless and aggressive, scrutinizing every soul in their path. Jeremiah's heart quickened, his determination momentarily disrupted by the harsh reality of oppression. The papers—Roman half-passports—rested against his chest, a tangible reminder of freedom in a world laden with chains.

He slowed, his presence now interwoven with the sobering reality of the times. Each step held weight as he approached the scrutiny of the Roman overseers. Fingers tightly clasped around the cherished document, Jeremiah steeled himself for the encounter, the fate of many hanging in the balance.

In the depths of slumber, Joseph found himself ensnared in a nightmarish visitation not orchestrated by the divine Gabriel, but by entities from the shadowy realms beneath. His peaceful rest became a battleground as malevolent messengers of the underworld invaded his subconscious, weaving a tapestry of deceit and temptation.

The demons whispered insidious lies into Joseph's vulnerable mind, painting a twisted narrative where Mary, his beloved, had betrayed their sacred bond. Fabricated tales of her supposed union with another man pervaded his dreams, and the weight of their deceit bore down on him. The sinister voices urged Joseph to take drastic action, to sacrifice Mary for the illusion of his own salvation.

Desperation clawed at Joseph's consciousness as he grappled with the surreal nightmare that held him captive. Attempts to awaken from this torment proved futile, the dreamlike realm trapping him in a sinister dance orchestrated by forces beyond comprehension. The ethereal chains of the underworld ensnared his senses, leaving Joseph to navigate a nightmarish landscape where truth and falsehood blurred into a disorienting maze.

As the demons continued their relentless assault, Joseph's mind became a battleground between the darkness that sought to corrupt and the flickering light of his unwavering love for Mary. The struggle persisted in the realm of dreams, testing the very fabric of his resolve and faith.

The three Magi, escorted through the lavish corridors adorned with intricate art and glistening gold, marveled at the opulence of Herod's palace. The king, seeking to display his grandeur, welcomed them with a facade of friendship, inquiring about their journey and the news of the prophesied newborn king.

With regal eloquence, the Magi recounted the ancient prophecy known to all the people of Yahweh, emphasizing the divine significance of the awaited Messiah. Herod, ever the cunning ruler, masked his lack of Torah knowledge and pretended to be well-versed in the prophecies. He cunningly invited the three men to reveal the location of the child once they found him, ostensibly to join in paying homage to this divine gift.

The Magi, wise to the king's machinations, diplomatically affirmed their dedication to the cause but skillfully evaded divulging any specifics. They assured Herod that, upon locating the child, they would dutifully return to share the joyous news. The kings, excusing themselves from the royal presence, were reunited with their belongings.

As they stepped out from the opulent chambers into the cool night air, a collective sigh of relief escaped the lips of the three men. Gazing skyward, they found solace and renewed guidance in the celestial lights that once again illuminated their path. The heavens, ever their celestial compass, continued to steer them toward the fulfillment of their divine quest.

As the sun dipped below the horizon, casting shadows over the landscape, Joseph found himself ensnared in a relentless struggle within the realm of his dreams. The forces of darkness whispered deceitful temptations, seeking to exploit the vulnerabilities of his human soul. Unseen battles waged in the depths of his subconscious, while Mary, ever-watchful, had been awake for hours, silently observing her husband's restless slumber.

However, the tranquility of the night was shattered when Mary's body convulsed in sudden agony. Her gasps were stifled by the intensity of the pain as her water broke, signaling the onset of the inevitable. Mary, now unable to endure the pain alone, knew she could no longer let Joseph remain in his troubled sleep.

In the quiet darkness of their makeshift camp, Mary gently reached out to Joseph, tenderly waking him from his tumultuous dreams. The gravity of the situation dawned on him as he emerged from the depths of his subconscious, and the urgency in Mary's eyes conveyed the impending arrival of a momentous event.

With the labor pains intensifying, Mary and Joseph faced the challenge together, their journey now taking an unexpected turn under the watchful gaze of the celestial lights that adorned the night sky. As the radiant stars bore witness to the unfolding miracle, a sense of divine presence enveloped the couple.

Chapter 8

Bethlehem

I n the encompassing darkness, Joseph hurriedly packed the camp, his hands moving with both urgency and tenderness. Mary, enduring the indescribable pain of childbirth, leaned against a rock for support. The celestial star overhead, a constant companion on their journey, cast a soft glow, illuminating the rugged terrain that lay ahead.

The couple pressed forward guided by the divine light, each step echoing the anticipation of a monumental event. The journey to Bethlehem was treacherous, a tumultuous ten miles fraught with the unseen forces that lurked in the shadows. It felt as if the very shadows and demons sensed the imminent arrival of the King of all Kings, and their presence intensified as Mary's pain intensified.

Every footfall was a testament to their faith, a defiance against the unseen adversaries that sought to disrupt this sacred pilgrimage. Mary's cries echoed through the hills, reaching the hidden crevices where shadows lurked. Yet, the celestial being within her seemed to stir the very fabric of the spiritual realm, a presence that the malevolent forces recoiled from.

Joseph, now a sentinel against both the physical and metaphysical threats, fought back the unseen demons that once haunted his dreams. They now manifested in the hills and mountains, observing the couple from the hidden folds of darkness. However, the radiant star above grew brighter, like a continued beacon of hope and protection.

As they approached Bethlehem, the star's brilliance intensified, casting away the encroaching darkness. The celestial light seemed to pierce through the veils of the spiritual realm, creating a sanctified path for the weary travelers.

Mary's cries of pain echoed through the narrow streets of Bethlehem as the contractions intensified with each passing moment. The celestial light from the guiding star overhead painted a surreal backdrop to this pivotal night, where the heavens seemed to converge with the earthly realm. The night had grown deep, and it must have been around 11:00 p.m. when they reached the gates of Bethlehem.

The next stage of their journey was to find a place for Mary to rest, a place where the divine child, the Son of God, would make His entrance into the world. Joseph, sensing the urgency, began to knock on the doors of fellow followers of Yahweh, seeking refuge for his beloved Mary. However, door after door remained closed, the occupants unwilling to offer shelter to strangers in the late hours.

Despite the rejections, Joseph pressed on, driven by a determination to find a sanctuary for Mary. As they continued knocking, a sense of desperation crept in, but Joseph knew they had to persevere. The image of his cousin Elijah's home offered a glimmer of hope, a haven of respite in his childhood home.

The journey through Bethlehem's streets felt like an eternity, Mary enduring the pangs of labor with unwavering strength. Finally, they reached the outskirts of Bethlehem, a humble farm that belonged to Joseph's relative, Elijah. Mary, now visibly in pain, found solace in the familiarity of family, even if it wasn't her own. Elijah's wife, Ishika, greeted them with warmth and compassion, ushering Mary into the comforting embrace of their dwelling. As Mary prepared to give birth, surrounded by the humble surroundings of Elijah's home, the stage was set for the miraculous arrival of the King of all Kings.

Inside the tent, the air was thick with a mixture of anticipation and warmth as Mary was carefully draped in layers of soft, comforting clothes by the compassionate women of Joseph's family. Each woman moved with purpose, their hands guided by a shared understanding of the sacredness of the moment. The flickering light of a small oil lamp cast a gentle glow, emphasizing the hushed reverence that enveloped the space.

Outside the tent, the farm seemed to respond to the profound event unfolding within its confines. The animals, normally bustling with life, gathered in a most extraordinary way. The sheep, the donkey, and even the fowl stood still, a silent congregation awaiting the birth of a child who held a destiny beyond their understanding.

Among the men, Joseph felt a heaviness in his heart. While surrounded by the familiarity of family and the echoes of days past in Bethlehem, there was no time for nostalgic remembrances. His attention was fully absorbed by the realization that Mary wasn't merely contending with the physical challenges of childbirth but was engaged in a cosmic battle against the forces of darkness that sought to prevent the arrival of this extraordinary child.

The night air resonated with Mary's rhythmic cries, and Joseph, along with the farm animals and the men, listened intently. Joseph wondered about Jeremiah, his younger cousin, who was on his way to join them. Would Jeremiah be there to witness the divine miracle unfolding before them?

Chapter 9

The Birth of a Savior

T he warmth that had enveloped the desert night suddenly gave way to a peculiar chill, and an uneasy stillness settled over the three Magi as they continued their journey. Melchior, the eldest among them, found himself caught off guard by the sudden disappearance of the celestial star that had faithfully guided them across the vast expanse of the desert.

Balthazar, his voice tinged with concern, sought answers, questioning the meaning behind this celestial shift. Jasper, ever solemn and wise, raised a hand, urging his companions to be silent, to open their eyes and ears to the divine guidance that transcended the visible world.

In the darkness, a revelation unfolded as the Magi discerned the presence of spies sent by King Herod to shadow their sacred journey. The gravity of the situation weighed heavily on their hearts, and a shared understanding passed among them—a realization that God, in His infinite wisdom, was issuing a warning.

Jasper, his countenance marked by solemn determination, spoke words that resonated with divine insight. He instructed his fellow Magi to alter their course, to travel in a direction opposite to the spies' pursuit. While this decision meant they might miss witnessing the miraculous birth of the King of all Kings, the Magi understood that it was an act in alignment with the divine will. They embraced the uncertainties that lay ahead, trusting that God's plan would unfold as ordained.

Jeremiah, carried effortlessly by divine momentum, arrived at the gates of Bethlehem just as the last stars of the night began to fade in the embrace of dawn. This town, unfamiliar to him, held the keys of his father's heritage, and he recognized that guidance from above would be crucial to locate his cousin Joseph in this bustling place.

The air was filled with a mixture of anticipation and trepidation as Jeremiah navigated through the narrow streets, guided by an intuition. He felt as though the very wings of God were gliding him through the unfamiliar paths, ensuring that he would reach his destination with purpose and grace.

Inside the tent, a sacred hush descended as Mary, surrounded by a circle of women, prepared for the imminent arrival of the divine child. The air was filled with a silent anticipation, and Mary, in a moment of serenity, spoke with a gentle authority, "For this will be the moment to bear witness as the son of God is welcomed into the world."

As her sentence trailed off, Mary's body, attuned to the rhythms of creation, began the final dance of labor. The women, silent witnesses to this miraculous event, offered their support and guidance as Mary braced herself for the sacred act of bringing forth life.

Outside the tent, Joseph and the men waited with bated breath, their anticipation heightened by the mysterious energy that enveloped the scene. Suddenly, a familiar face appeared—a young boy with brown, tousled hair and a dirt-streaked face. Joseph's heart recognized him instantly as his cousin Jeremiah.

In that pivotal moment, the air crackled with a symphony of sounds—a chorus of animal cries, the rustling of leaves, and the ethereal echo of a newborn's first cry. The atmosphere resonated with a divine presence, signaling the momentous occasion that the Messiah had been born. The very fabric of Bethlehem seemed to tremble in awe as the world welcomed the long-awaited King.

As if struck by a divine dagger, all three Magi fell to their knees at the very moment of the Messiah's birth. Overwhelmed by the celestial energy that permeated the air, tears streamed down their faces. It was as if the King of all Kings had entered the world, a sacred gift from God to His people—a beacon of light destined to lead the Israelites out of darkness.

A great sand tornado spiraled around the Magi, forming a protective barrier that sent the spies, shadows sent by Herod, spinning far away. Their malevolent gaze and intent were lost in the tempest, leaving the Magi free from the prying eyes of Herod's envoys. Jasper, the sage among them, looked at his fellow companions with a knowing gaze and spoke with an air of wisdom, "From where we stand, it is an eight-day journey." The others, puzzled yet trusting in Jasper's insights, understood that this whisper of knowledge was a guidance from the divine.

In the humble surroundings of the farm, the sacred rituals of birth unfolded seamlessly. The attendees, women with hands weathered by time and hearts filled with ancestral wisdom, moved with a grace that spoke of years spent in service to the ancient customs. Each step in the ritual held profound significance, a connection to generations past and a bridge to the divine.

The cutting of the umbilical cord was a delicate dance, a symbol of the separation between mother and child, marking the beginning of an independent journey. The newborn, wrapped in a blanket of familial love, was then tenderly washed with water, a cleansing act that mirrored the spiritual purity of the moment. The attendants, their movements deliberate and filled with purpose, carefully rubbed the child with purifying salt, bestowing blessings upon the newborn in a tradition as old as time.

As the sacred practices continued, the small tent became a sanctuary where earthly and divine converged. Swaddled in the simple yet profound act of clothing the baby, the child was adorned with the essence of tradition. The air, heavy with the scent of incense and the echoes of ancient prayers, carried the weight of centuries of childbirth rituals, binding the present moment to the sacred tapestry of the past.

In the serene aftermath of the sacred rituals, the time arrived for the significant act of naming the newborn. The parents, Mary and Joseph, stood together with an air of solemnity, their eyes reflecting the gravity of the moment. The attendants, aware of the profound importance of this tradition, awaited the chosen name with bated breath.

Joseph, with a sense of paternal pride and a heart open to divine guidance, gazed down at the child cradled in Mary's arms. Mary, her countenance glowing with a blend of exhaustion and elation, looked upon her son, feeling the weight of responsibility mingled with boundless love. Together, in a hushed whisper that resonated with spiritual resonance, they chose the name for their newborn: Jesus.

The syllables of the name seemed to carry an otherworldly grace, echoing through the humble tent and resonating with the ancestral spirits that surrounded them. The attendants, witnesses to this sacred act of naming, understood that Jesus was more than just a name; it was a beacon of hope, a promise, and a vessel for the divine purpose that had brought them all together.

As the chosen name graced the air, the newborn Jesus seemed to respond with a quiet serenity, as if acknowledging the weight of the destiny that awaited him.

In this simple yet profound act of naming, the child became more than an earthly presence; he became a symbol of divine intervention, a beacon of light heralding the arrival of a new era. The small tent, filled with the essence of tradition, love, and reverence, held the echo of a name that would resonate through history and carry the hopes of generations to come.

Chapter 10

Three Kings

I n the radiant glow of the Bethlehem night, the celestial star stood as a sentinel, guiding the three Magi towards their destined arrival at Elijah's humble farmhouse. Jasper, overcome with awe and reverence, couldn't suppress the melody that welled up within him, and soon his voice resonated in a sacred song, echoing through the quiet town.

As they approached the dwelling, the star's luminous presence seemed to intensify, casting a divine glow over Elijah's abode. The men, recognizing the culmination of their journey, felt a profound sense of purpose. With grateful hearts, they knelt before Mary, who cradled the newborn Jesus, the King of all Kings, in her arms.

The timing of their arrival was impeccable, marking the eighth day since Jesus's birth—a sacred juncture for the ritual of circumcision. The three wise men, guided by both tradition and divine revelation, proceeded to carry out the sacred Jewish ceremony. Each step was executed with utmost reverence, as they bestowed their holy gifts upon the infant.

Jeremiah, witnessing the culmination of prophecies and miracles, had his beliefs affirmed. The convergence of the celestial star, the sacred ritual, and the presence of the Messiah marked this night as an extraordinary moment in the tapestry of divine intervention. As they fulfilled their sacred duties, the men couldn't help but feel the weight of their purpose, their gifts serving as both earthly treasures and symbolic gestures of homage to the King of all Kings.

On the 9th night after Jesus's birth, both Jasper and Joseph were granted premonitory dreams by the angel

Gabriel. In the realm of dreams, Jasper received a divine message, clear and unwavering—he and his companions were not to return to Herod. The celestial emissary urged them to keep the location of Jesus's miraculous birth a secret, and instead, they were to embark on an alternate route, traversing through different lands and eventually crossing the Red Sea.

Meanwhile, Joseph's dream unfolded in vivid scenes, saturated with an undercurrent of fear. Unlike the shadowy apparitions he had encountered in the desert, these visions were unambiguous signs from God. Gabriel spoke directly to Joseph, instructing him to gather Mary and the infant Jesus swiftly. The urgency in the angel's message was palpable—Herod's intentions were malicious, a looming threat that could only be thwarted by immediate action. The divine directive was clear: Joseph was to lead his family to safety by escaping to the sanctuary of Egypt.

As the morning sun painted the sky with hues of gold and amber, both Jasper and Joseph found themselves reluctant to share the foreboding visions that had visited them in the night. The air was thick with unspoken apprehension, yet a shared understanding lingered between them—the time for celebration had drawn to a close, and the weight of their divine directives pressed upon their hearts.

As the three kings prepared to depart, the air became charged with a sense of purpose. With a deep reverence, they presented their sacred gifts to Joseph and Mary, tokens of homage for the newborn King. In solemn tones, they foretold of the treacherous path that lay ahead for the Holy Family and spoke of their own intention to journey, proclaiming the advent of the newly born King to the children of God in foreign lands.

Joseph and Mary, sensing the gravity of their situation, decided to linger for one more evening in the familiar embrace of Bethlehem before undertaking the arduous journey through Egypt. Jeremiah, gazing upon his beloved cousin Joseph, recognized the weight of their impending separation.

As the night unfolded, Jeremiah and Joseph engaged in heartfelt conversation, their words punctuated by the blessings of a friend parting ways with kin. Jeremiah, in his sincerity, bestowed blessings upon Joseph, Mary, and the divine infant, acknowledging the challenges that lay ahead on their sacred journey. Each word carried the weight of unspoken goodbyes, for Joseph and Jeremiah knew that the shifting sands of destiny were propelling them into different realms.

With the moon casting its silvery glow upon Bethlehem, Joseph, Mary, and the newborn set forth on their journey under the cover of night, leaving behind the hallowed ground where the Messiah had made his earthly debut. The landscape transformed as they ventured into the unknown, a poignant reminder that their world had irrevocably changed with the birth of the holy child.

Upon realizing the perceived treachery committed against him, Herod's wrath erupted like a tempest within the confines of his palace. The spies he had dispatched had returned with only vague information, knowing merely that the three wise men had headed toward Bethlehem but lacking the specific location of the child who posed a threat to Herod's reign. The king, overcome by a furious determination, threw a tantrum that reverberated through the opulent halls of his palace.

In his resolve, which would be remembered as unforgiving and villainous, Herod devised a heinous plan to secure his throne. That fateful night, consumed by a paranoid fear of losing his grip on power, Herod decreed a merciless and unspeakable edict. In an act of unspeakable horror, he ordered that all male infants aged two years or younger in Bethlehem and its surrounding cities were to be massacred, a grotesque sacrifice intended to extinguish any perceived threat to his eternal rule.

The chilling decree reflected Herod's desperation and ruthlessness, as he sought to eliminate any potential rivals to his throne, even if it meant the slaughter of innocent children. The air in Bethlehem, once filled with the joyous echoes of a miraculous birth, now hung heavy with the impending darkness of a tyrant's merciless decree.

Chapter 11

A Rush To Salvation

The cries of men and women echoed through the narrow streets of Bethlehem, a haunting symphony of anguish and despair. Herod's merciless decree had come to fruition, and his men descended upon the town like harbingers of darkness. They executed the sinister order with ruthless efficiency, leaving behind a trail of horror and heartbreak.

Innocent blood stained the cobblestone streets as the soldiers massacred every male infant they encountered. The once joyful and vibrant town was now transformed into a nightmarish scene, with the wails of grieving mothers piercing the air. The tears flowed freely, a river of sorrow carved by the tragic loss of young lives.

Mothers clutched their infants tightly, their protective instincts unable to shield their precious ones from the brutality that unfolded. The cruel decree cast a shadow over Bethlehem, turning the joyous echoes of a miraculous birth into a symphony of sorrow and mourning. The streets, once filled with the laughter of children, were now painted with the indelible stain of a tyrant's brutality. The cries of anguish reverberated, a lamentation for the innocent lives taken too soon.

The once serene farmhouse of Elijah, a place that held memories of solace and remembrance, was now marred by the gruesome brutality inflicted by the Roman guards. The crimson stain of innocent blood adorned the walls, a stark contrast to the beauty that once filled its halls. Jeremiah, scarred by the horrifying sight of Elijah's three young children lying lifeless, felt the weight of despair settle over him.

In the face of such unspeakable tragedy, Jeremiah's heart pounded with grief, and an overwhelming urge to flee from the horrors that unfolded before him took hold. He scattered through his possessions, hastily collecting whatever he could carry, the echoes of the cries of the fallen children haunting his every step.

With the devastation of Bethlehem behind him, Jeremiah ran, his breaths ragged, leaving the once-holy town to its sorrow. The cries of his fellow men and women of God lingered in the air, a painful reminder of the suffering that had befallen them. As he fled, Jeremiah couldn't shake the profound realization that the prophecy that brought Jesus to the land was intertwined with the tragic destiny of his people, born from the crucible of suffering.

In the tranquil refuge far from the reaches of Herod's malevolence and even further from the border of Egypt, Joseph and Mary, oblivious to the harrowing actions unfolding in Bethlehem, found solace and gratitude in the divine guidance that had steered their path. The baby Jesus, nestled peacefully in Mary's arms, emanated an air of serenity that seemed to bless the journey ahead.

With a mother's tender gaze, Mary looked upon her son, a living testament to the divine providence that had led them through tumultuous landscapes and perilous circumstances. The knowledge that all was unfolding as it should, according to the divine plan, filled her heart with a profound sense of gratitude.

Joseph, the gifted carpenter, embraced his role with grace and skill. Crafting a beautiful cradle from the humble manger that once held Jesus in Elijah's home, he created a symbol of love, protection, and the resilience that would be required in the days to come. Both Mary and Joseph, in the quiet moments between the coos and cries of their newborn, understood the gravity of the task that lay ahead.

As Jeremiah's frantic run continued, the haunting image of Elijah's tear-streaked face lingered in his mind. The weight of witnessing the massacre of Elijah's family, his innocent sons torn away from him, fueled Jeremiah's urgency. Each step seemed to echo the cries of the wailing mothers, blending with the sobs of grieving fathers, creating a cacophony of despair that resonated through the air.

His relentless pace was abruptly halted by the sudden appearance of Roman slave traders. Their demand for Jeremiah's papers, the proof of his Roman citizenship, pierced through the chaos of his thoughts. Panic surged within him as he fumbled through his belongings, realizing with a sinking feeling that he must have left the crucial documents behind in Elijah's home in the midst of the massacre.

With this revelation, the atmosphere thickened with tension. The harsh thud of a blunt force against the back of Jeremiah's head echoed through the air. As he crumpled to the ground, the unforgiving sands of Judea slipped through his grasp, marking the beginning of an unforeseen and perilous journey into the unknown.

In the heart of Egypt, Mary and Joseph embarked on a journey that stretched across the vast landscapes, far from the tormented echoes of Bethlehem. Joseph, with the knowledge of distant relatives residing in the bustling Greek colony and Roman stronghold of Alexandria, guided his family towards this grand city—a place where they could find refuge amidst the anonymity of urban life while still remaining close to the divine presence of Yahweh.

The sounds of Alexandria, a symphony of labor and

construction, reverberated through the air. The tang of sea salt from the nearby Mediterranean danced on the breeze, reaching the senses of Mary and Joseph as they entered the city. It was here, amidst the labyrinthine streets and towering structures, that they sought solace and the promise of a new beginning. Alexandria, with its grandeur and anonymity, held the potential for Mary and Joseph to forge a life away from the shadows of Herod's wrath.

Chapter 12

13 Years

Ａs the sun began to cast its golden glow over the rocky seascape, a young man in his twenties, his brown hair tousled from the gentle breeze, slowly opened his eyes. His hands, though marked with a minuscule amount of labor, retained a certain softness. Dressed in Roman attire, he lay on the uneven surface, awakening to the rhythmic melody of the sea below.

His companion, a slender man with Roman heritage, possessed striking features—a cascade of blonde hair and piercing blue eyes. He sat beside the young man, gazing at him with a look of reverence. The tranquility of the sea enveloped them, broken only by the mellifluous voice of the blonde man as he called out to his companion by name.

"We have almost reached the shores, Jeremiah." The words carried a sense of anticipation, a promise of the imminent arrival at their destination.

As Jeremiah, now in his early twenties, gazed upon the land that he called home, a sense of determination and purpose filled his heart. He turned to the young blonde man standing beside him, a companion in this journey of faith and destiny, and spoke with unwavering resolve.

"Our work has just begun," he declared. The words hung in the air, carrying the weight of the trials and tribulations he had faced, the prophecies he had witnessed, and the miracles that had unfolded.

Jeremiah, bound by a shared destiny and a profound connection to the divine, now stood on the precipice of a new chapter. The land before him held the echoes of Yahweh's guidance, and he was ready to embark on the sacred work that awaited him. With a sense of purpose and the strength of faith, he stepped forward, united in their commitment to the divine plan that had shaped his life. The sun dipped below the horizon, casting a warm glow, marking the beginning of a new phase in his journey.

About The Author

Robert Jerome Pagan

Robert Jerome Pagan has been immersed in biblical narratives since his early years, where his Catholic roots were deeply embedded through active participation in vacation bible schools and spreading the word of the Lord. In his youth, he assumed the role of a minister, finding joy in the profound beauty encapsulated within the Bible. As he transitioned into adulthood, Pagan's involvement in theater and film provided him with insights into the cultural impact and interconnectedness shared by tradition.

Driven by a steadfast belief that Jesus' mission was rooted in love and acceptance rather than hatred, Pagan felt compelled to narrate the story of Jesus through a fresh perspective. Although new to the realm of novels, his dedication to conveying the significance of the tale of Joseph and Mary is well-established, as evidenced by his award-winning film, " An American Posada."

Made in the USA
Columbia, SC
25 July 2024

38838814R00052